How to Stop Looking Autistic

Autism

Greg Stucky

Published by Greg Stucky, 2020.

While every precaution has been taken in the preparation of this book, the publisher assumes no responsibility for errors or omissions, or for damages resulting from the use of the information contained herein.

HOW TO STOP LOOKING AUTISTIC

First edition. March 5, 2020.

Copyright © 2020 Greg Stucky.

ISBN: 979-8201679699

Written by Greg Stucky.

Table of Contents

How to Stop Looking Autistic

Greg Stucky

How to Stop Looking Autistic by Greg Stucky

© 2019 Greg Stucky

Second Edition

All Rights Reserved

No portion of this book may be reproduced in any form without permission from the publisher, except as permitted by US. copyright law. For permissions contact:

greg@stucky.tech

Visit the author's website at https://stucky.tech.

Other Books by this Author:

- How to Start Looking at Autism

Websites by this Author:

- https://stucky.tech
- https://adequate.life
- https://gainedin.site
- https://theologos.site
- https://entertaining.space

To my neurotypical wife, who endured an atypical amount of patience with me.

Why I'm Writing This

For most of history, autism wasn't a thing. Even today, it's still difficult to define. By misunderstanding facts, people respond poorly. I write this because I want to set the facts straight.

Unlike most other psychological diagnoses, Autism Spectrum Disorder (ASD) places history's celebrities right next to people with special needs and socially awkward people. From the outside, neurotypicals often imagine ASD's vague definition includes anyone with poor social skills. From the autistics I've talked to, they're justifiably confused about what the diagnosis means to them.

I want people with ASD to see what their condition is, in plain English. Often, modern society labels someone who suffers as a hero. ASD, however, needs the plain facts more than most people. The built-in gift of autism, probably more than anyone else, is that we see the world for what it *is* and must work our way into what others *see* it as.

My situation is unique for this purpose. I was a mid-functioning autistic in my formative years and hadn't received any formal autism diagnosis or therapy when I was young. Since most of society hadn't given much attention to autism, I thought I was defective. I didn't realize I had a diagnosis that would follow me for the rest of my life.

I worked hard to conform to "normal". I wanted others to respect me and listen to my ideas. I've now attained it, and this book is designed to give you the same success.

You won't ever be "normal". The label is impossible because of how your brain works. However, you *can* become a high functioning autistic. If you push past self-prescribed victimhood, people will call you "creative", "interesting", "fascinating", "revolutionary", or even "life-changing". It takes work, but it's 100% possible.

Nobody has probably told you this, but autism is dangerous to diagnose. The very nature of autism is to over-identify with things, and I've seen too many self-diagnosed ASD who expect things to change merely by labeling themselves with ASD.

ASD has many strengths, but you must learn to channel them. The reason names like Bill Gates or Philo Farnsworth resonate well in society is because those people focused more on achieving than in finding acceptance. Then, the acceptance came later.

Remember that you're *not* alone. If we could measure everyone on the spectrum, I imagine about 10% of the planet is autistic. If we zoomed in on technical jobs in STEM, history, writing, and accounting I'm almost certain that number would spike to 40%!

More than anything, I want you to walk away with one idea. Autism is *not* a "disorder", nor is it a mental illness. When wielded correctly, it's a strength. Some of my greatest achievements came from wrapping myself in the minutiae and ignoring the big picture. So, for the rest of the book I'm calling it AS, not ASD.

This book isn't for everyone. If you want to know how to survive, this book won't help you. I'm writing to you if you're on the spectrum and tired of feeling inexplicably inferior among your peers. Most AS will naïvely sabotage their credibility without knowing it, but nobody ever takes the time to teach them otherwise. By the end of this book, I promise you'll know which nonverbals to focus on and the general reasoning behind them.

As of my writing this, I don't think anyone else is communicating it like I am. Most neurotypicals aren't aware of their own behavior and presume everyone else is thinking the way they are.

If you know you're not autistic or not sure, I recommend my parallel book: *How to Start Looking at Autism*. It's built for neurotypicals in understanding the prevalent, quirky minority that breaks most social statistics. For the rest of you, onward to the facts!

What Autism Is

Autism is now a buzzword. Movies and TV like *Rain Man*, *Extremely Loud and Incredibly Close*, and *Silicon Valley* clarify how autism looks. Unfortunately, visual media often fails to show how the mechanism of how autism thinks.

No single behavior can track AS, which is frustrating for most people because they want a quick solution. Since they're not willing to examine more deeply, the average person finds autism an impossible mystery. To compensate for their non-knowing, psychologists blended autism with Asperger's Syndrome and called it ASD.

Autism has plenty of qualitative data, but very little quantitative. While there's a childhood test, psychologists haven't created a formal ASD test for adults. Since scientists have very little confirmation about how AS thinks or even how it happens, all the proposed therapies and solutions are holistic guesses.

The purpose here isn't to change how you think. Successfully navigating with autism requires merely changing attitude and behavior. However, if you understand how you think, you'll have an easier time understanding what you do.

How Autism Thinks

Autism spectrum (AS) has a completely different neurology that neurotypicals (NT). Most NTs don't understand AS unless they've spent time around them. I've placed the popular diagnoses in **bold** to emphasize my reasoning.

This is the simplest "autism test" I know of. NTs see large letters and zoom down to the small ones. AS sees the small letters first, then build up their relationships into the large ones.

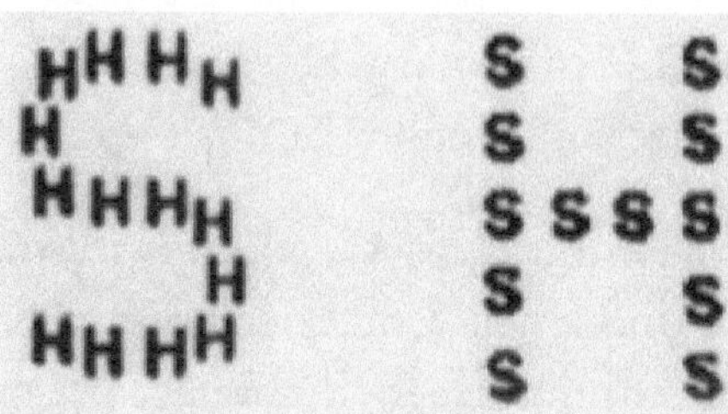

To paraphrase Temple Grandin, the autistic mind attends to details while the normal brain ignores them.

People start "chunking" from infancy. Chunking is grouping small things together into patterns that become summarized larger things. A baby, for example, will learn that 3 connected lines is a triangle and 4 connected lines is a square. Genetic or environmental factors will give a child **difficulty chunking things**.

Human brains receive a tidal wave of information, assign values, throw most of it away, then store copies of what's left. An AS child's poor chunking means they have a hard time prioritizing, so they store far more "junk" information. Since they can't rank information nearly as quickly, they're **hypersensitive and/or insensitive to stimuli**. Too much information at once will overload them (also known as **over-stimulation**).

To cope with **stimming**, AS children often create fixed objects as "givens". Givens can be the order of things in a physical space, a familiar object, a certain method, or anything else that feels familiar. It's a useful coping mechanism but requires the environment to comply, and they'll likely feel **over-stimulation when a given thing changes**.

Beyond mental coping mechanisms, AS also use behaviors to cope with the stimming. Since the eyes convey a *lot* of information, most of them have **trouble making eye contact**. They will often self-soothe with **repetitive behaviors/activities or repeat words**. They may focus on external givens like **spinning objects** or **self-harm** in extreme situations.

In interpersonal and performance situations, AS usually understand they must meet expectations they don't know and often battle **extreme anxiety**. That stress creates a variety of **tics**.

AS escape the information overload with **sub-niche interests** (e.g., whales, 19th century Scotch literature) with little interest in related subjects (e.g., dolphins, 17th century Scotch literature). The niche interest is a subconscious desire for a small, controllable world without an endless deluge of details.

AS children can't "automate" thought well (goes back to chunking) and **learn specific subjects slower than other children**. They'll develop an irregular pattern of competencies ("**splintering**"). Some of them have spectacular gifts (a "**savant**"). They'll also suffer **poor coordination** that may hamper their abilities in athletics or physical labor.

AS doesn't process feelings easily. Emotions are overwhelming for them, so their subconscious usually copes with **numbness to feelings**. Since they're generally ignoring their feelings, they usually have **trouble expressing feelings**.

Compulsive and impulsive behaviors are harder to resist without emotional awareness. AS are usually also **oblivious to others' feelings** or thoughts (**"mind-blindness"**). This unawareness may even go as far as **oblivious that others have differing viewpoints and presumptions**. This creates **frequent, consistent, inappropriate social experiences** and **trouble finding meaning in groups**.

Some of them easily understand challenging subjects while failing to grasp common-sense ideas. Their **lack of common sense** usually gets them in trouble. Anyone, not only AS, with a consistent record of failing at basic tasks would *naturally* battle **chronic depression**.

Scientists have sub-classed AS neurology into three major groups. **Visual thinkers** perfectly store and recall images. **Pattern thinkers** find connections between unrelated elements. **Verbal thinkers** masterfully manipulate language and words. Some AS can do more than one of these, but they all dominate with one of them. A visual thinker could be terrible at math or a verbal thinker might not be able to imagine a picture.

AS Has Advantages

If you're AS, you have an unusual skill at visualizing, finding patterns or using words. If you've been labeling yourself AS you're likely focusing on what you're failing at more than your natural gifts. Though focusing on our faults is human nature, we only succeed when we focus on answers.

The rest of this book will tell you very explicitly *how* to conform well enough for people to not see you as autistic. You have a unique and interesting perspective that most people should hear. In fact, most NTs you'll encounter find your views fascinating if they can get past how you're behaving. Instead of waiting for the masses to change for you, you'll need to adapt to their prejudices and expectations if you want to connect with them.

Many Unwritten Rules

Most NTs understand the importance of socializing. AS, though, often fail to understand its impact. Most of them usually find workarounds to live without human interaction.

NTs concern themselves far more about what *appears to be* than what *is*. Most of them see the image of things, then don't see any further. While different groups call it optics, image or narrative, it's all about the appearance of things far more than what reality shows.

AS rarely pay attention to the image they convey. Thus, most of the NT world is perplexed by them.

Thousands of social rules exist in society. Every single one has a reason for existing, though most people don't really ask why. Most people honor the rules to gain favor with everyone else.

I call this series of social rules the "human interaction system", or HIS. It's a series of telegraphed behaviors people respond back-and-forth with other people. Everyone judges people as "fit" or "unfit" with this system, but they usually do it subconsciously.

The HIS always concerns itself with what people *ought* to do and rarely with what people *can* do.

Here's an example of what an AS may observe in a social exchange:

A hot dog vendor is yelling "Fresh hot dogs here!" A man says, "One, please." He pays for the hot dog, then the vendor grimaces as he hands the man the hot dog.

Here's a sample of an NT observing the same thing:

A hot dog vendor is selling his hot dogs when a man walks up with a swagger. When the man asks for a hot dog, he leans forward on the counter and speaks with a loud, demanding voice. The vendor's eyes dart around because of the public attention he's drawing. In his anxiety, the vendor grimaces to show his disgust at the public spectacle and thrusts the hot dog at the man.

AS rarely misses details, but we often neglect to observe the *right* social details. This is because social interactions are fraught with many useless details. There are so many rules and counter-rules that we get confused us on *which* details to focus on. Since most NTs do this by sheer habit before they could talk, they're usually unsettled by AS behaviors.

The HIS is maddening for us because context determines all human expressions. Subtle, profound differences rely on hundreds of variables. These variables include who you're with, how many people you're talking to, the time of day, and the venue or your geographic location. Plus, each person has their own exceptions and caveats to these rules.

One of the most frustrating HIS rules is that people usually aren't supposed to talk about most of the rules. For example, if someone is selling my friend a bad product, I'm not allowed to voice my problems with the product while the seller is present. As another example, if you greet someone and they don't greet you back, it's usually rude to ask why they didn't greet you.

Another irritating rule is that people should shame anyone who doesn't follow the HIS. Even people who wouldn't shun you otherwise might worry about their reputation. I won't talk about shame in this book, but understand that it's a complicated social procedure that AS will likely never understand.

This non-disclosure of the rules is most of the reason NTs confuse us. For example, an NT who thinks you've been blunt or loud will ask for you to "tone it down a bit" but won't clarify an appropriate level or explain why. Polite correction only works when social skills are second nature. They're trying to teach social algebra when we don't understand social arithmetic.

The HIS is unreliable and unpredictable. NTs still honor it because they have enough trust issues that they need to investigate everyone they encounter but don't have time to be thorough. Many people who can game the social system (e.g., sleazy sales, con artists) create false positives, which then leads to more distrust.

You probably hate the HIS, and it's natural to be angry at it. If you're reading this book, the system probably labels you consistently as a false negative.

Unfortunately, you won't achieve much by expecting everyone to cater to your needs. Even if you try to increase awareness, most people don't care enough to change themselves. Since you're the one most hurt by this failed communication, you have more reason to change.

HIS will be with us forever. It's how humans interact, so we must grit our teeth and work this defective system to our purposes. It's your only hope of connection, financial wellness, success, friendships or feeling "normal". Fighting it will leave you alone with a small handful of other rebels, but learning it guarantees you'll find meaning and importance.

While NTs trust their intuition and sharpen it with experience and feelings, AS needs a different system. While AS are more rigid to changes than NTs, they have a hidden advantage.

AS have better memories than NTs. If you observe something and successfully encode it, you can vividly remember it *years* afterward. By contrast, NT memories are hazy and vague. They must routinely revisit old ideas to refresh them.

Also, AS lives by rhythmic consistency. Most NTs get bored or distracted easily, but AS are natural prodigies at anything they set their minds to. Thus, if you know what to do and why it's worth it, you'll have a much easier time doing it.

AS success in the NT world is making your public expressions, mannerisms, reactions, and body language into a performance. While you can completely lower your guard around people you trust in private, your success hinges on your public image. Trust me when I say it isn't as hard as it sounds.

If You Disagree

Many AS will find this advice wrong or even offensive. Why "lie" to others about what you are? Why deceive everyone to "fit in"? What right does the rest of society have determining what you can and can't do with your own body?

I spent years wrestling with that conflict. I tried showing my raw aptitude but kept changing or losing jobs because I offended people. People care more about how they feel about you than what you know. I've learned that everyone consumes themselves with the need to feel important. You can't tell people they're wrong until they know you have a genuine desire for their well-being.

I hoped I could escape the pervasive effects of HIS by drilling into a career niche (accounting, in my case). I figured a respectable job would make people look more at what I did than how I conveyed myself. Unfortunately, managers will only hire employees they like because they must work alongside them. While you might find work, you'll only find true job security with a good reputation.

No matter where I went, I wanted to be true to myself but also wanted to do what everyone else expected. After many conversations with NTs, I found that they have the same identity conflicts as AS on a much smaller scale. Many of them can't self-identify without social affiliations or hobbies.

The sociologist Erving Goffman once made the claim that we are nothing *but* our performed selves. You call yourself "you", but how much of that is *really* you and how much did you borrow from your upbringing or environment?

AS often imitates people and things. A well-formed AS can swap out inspirations seamlessly enough that an NT will never really notice. Some of the most well-known AS creatives use this to great effect.

Human interaction is at the core of everything we do. The ideas of Socrates and Aristotle are merely written works passed down from people. Computers are logic machines made by people. We anthropomorphize our experiences onto animals and over-presume their "human-ness". To remove humanity is to remove ourselves.

We only find meaning in how we connect with others. If you feel bitter about needing to build a performance for other people to accept you, think how an NT feels. They've been living and thinking with the HIS their whole life! While you can switch the HIS on and off after you've learned it, they can't.

When they get past their initial distrust, the world embraces blatant authenticity. Since AS usually has trouble lying about small things, they're already expressing their authentic self! If AS can work through NTs' hesitancy to trust, nothing can stop them!

I'm not saying for you to have empathy with the rest of the world, but you must have more patience with them. Masquerading as an NT when you're AS is a test of perpetual restraint. You'll need to bite your tongue, keep your thoughts and feelings to yourself, and let people persist in believing dumb ideas.

Is it worth it? That's up to you to decide. Check out Tim Burton or Dan Aykroyd. Their ideas and expressions are world-famous because they kept most of their unpopular ideas to themselves. Choose what hill you want to die on.

You CAN Do It

For us, social skills will always be a second language. You'll never understand social rules well enough to be "normal". Most people hit about 95% of the HIS rules without trying. At about 90%, people will completely write off tics and stimming as idiosyncrasies. Mainstream society will judge you as eccentric (as opposed to crazy) if you can perform at least 85% of the HIS rules. By my estimation, mid functioning AS hits 60-80% of the HIS rules without trying!

Your single-minded passion is one of your greatest assets. AS have a remarkable ability to focus on a project with unwavering diligence. Many of them short sell their ability because they either thought their obsession was normal or they noticed that society finds it intimidating.

To get social skills right, you *must* extend your interests into the public realm. If you're a normal AS, one of the most difficult questions to answer is "what *do* you like?" Though you aren't labeling yourself as "liking" something, for all intents and purposes you "like" something if you do it all the time.

Identify with your interests. You might like one of the sciences like biology, physics or chemistry. You might have esoteric interests with a sub-sub-field like archaeology or botany. You might love entertainment like video games, movies or television. You might enjoy a fictional world like the Marvel or DC Universe, Star Wars, Middle Earth, Star Trek, Doctor Who or Discworld.

Though you weren't paying attention, you're probably among the top 10% most knowledgeable on that subject. You engrossed yourself in something for many hours. You're an expert in the subject without even doing anything that felt like work!

We learn what we love, and AS usually falls madly in love with special interests. We're driven to learn those interests so much, in fact, that high functioning AS uses those interests as a framework to understand the world.

You must treat socializing with the same passion as that interest. If you believe you can live without people, you're severely overestimating yourself. We need people for everything, from physical needs to finding meaning. To disassociate from our need for people is to become less human.

Whatever your passion is, find an analogy from it to describe your social issues. I tend to think of people as complicated computers with ridiculous subroutines. When I was an accountant, I imagined social skills as a type of asset management.

- If you're into biology, humans are a specific, complicated species.
- If you play video games, life is a game with rules and objectives and a missing instruction book.
- If you're into movies or television, life is a very long movie or show with the best characters and most intricate plot.
- If you're into Star Wars, relationships are the Force that binds us together and brings unseen changes.
- If you draw or paint, conversations are a painting made by multiple people on the canvas of time.
- If you build things like LEGOs or robots, relationships are a brick-by-brick structure or schematic.
- If you play music, communication is a song with multiple musicians.
- If you like chemistry, human interactions are a reaction with behaviors catalyzing everything.
- If you like computer networking, people are independent nodes with unreliable channels and conflicting protocols.

I can't give every single one because it would require 5,000 pages! Every AS is creative once they have clear rules. Form the rules from your favorite analogy, then adapt them as you discover things that don't fit that analogy.

One minor note of caution. I have encountered several AS (and was once one) who tried to force the world's rules to conform with my *system's* model. Let the world's rules define the thought-based model and *not* the other way around or you *will* lose your mind.

You learned your hobby's intricacies and exceptions because you were passionate about it, so socializing is the same thing. Tackle interactions with other people the same way.

Slice your social life into small enough pieces to conduct experiments. When you're not 100% certain everyone was comfortable with your behavior, drill down. Make each engagement, conversation, statement, word, and gesture worth a thorough investigation. Reproduce actions with different people, times, places, and circumstances to build an accurate predictive model.

Write out rules and make a system. Get detailed! Create rules from what you already know and change them as you discover new facts. Make guidelines on how the world works from what you're already familiar with. AS intuition is finicky, but finely sharpened "gut" instincts are the most powerful human reasoning system humanity has!

Don't expect NTs to help you much. Most of them run all their routines subconsciously, so anything you learn will likely be news to *them*! You're venturing into things everyone else has unwittingly ignored!

If you don't think it's worth it, don't waste your time with the rest of the book. If you think you've gotten a good analogy to plug new facts into, the next chapter will give you some good starting rules.

The Biggest Social Rules

Most of the following rules are largely non-negotiable. You might be able to break some of them on occasion, but people will run you out of town if you break too many.

As you learn the HIS, dedicated practice will turn these ideas into habits. While it might feel impossible right now, your AS makes you an unusually quick study if you're motivated.

Just remember that you don't always have to understand *why* something is a social rule to honor it. Once you're familiar with it enough, you can learn when to break it for a profound impact. Successful artists, musicians, and comedians know exactly when and how to break rules. Until then, play it safe and make honoring the rule a baseline.

If we get down to the reasoning, many of the purposes for these rules are irrational or ridiculous. NTs are naturally fearful, anxious and prone to prejudice. They also abide by logic based on experiences that are completely alien to you. They see things top-down and you see them bottom-up.

I've given a few theories interspersed in these rules. Most of the HIS rules arose because everyone imitated the quirks of someone important. Every one of the rules was designed to address someone's feelings.

Take on the rules one at a time. Observe people in public places and note what they do and avoid. Work step by step to understand them enough to integrate them into your routine. Often, you'll find that those dumb rules are to accommodate people who are less rational than you.

One admonition: try to avoid learning from fiction. People use movies, TV, video games, and novels to stir up the strongest emotions possible. They're commentary on reality, *not* reality itself. Real-life expressions aren't as flamboyant or odd, so don't use fiction as a reference point.

Also, knowledge gives power. You'll quickly discover that people you thought were your friends weren't. As you build your skills, you may even out-succeed your friends. The good friends will stick around and change their role, but you'll lose favor with the bad friends.

I must also warn you of other AS and their behaviors. Other people breaking the HIS won't matter now, but you'll notice as you habituate yourself to proper conduct how blatantly many AS violate the social rules. Let them live the way they want and focus on yourself.

Preparing for Socializing

Great social experiences appear spontaneous, but professional engagers will plan them out. Most people, in general, don't plan for their social engagements, but your preparation compensates for your weaknesses.

Every time you leave your home, expect to have a conversation with someone. Always clean yourself before leaving. Bathe or shower, brush your hair and teeth, and trim or remove any unwanted body hair.

Since your nose acclimates to your body odor, clean more than you think you'll need. Wear a light scenting of perfume or cologne if it doesn't stim you. Only apply enough that someone can smell it if they're hugging you. Since your nose gets accustomed to that as well, only apply once.

When dressing, try to dress with the same outfits as everyone else. If you want, err with clothing a little nicer than everyone else, but expect to draw attention. Coordinate colors and patterns to complement your skin color. Use a color wheel online if you need complementary colors. There are entire books on this subject alone.

Prepare small talk questions in advance. Most of the world treats small talk as a "trial run" to experiment without commitment. AS is usually terrible at small talk.

You have many small talk examples to choose from. Give genuine compliments on anything except someone's body. Ask general topics about someone's school or workplace. Ask about their hobbies and interests. Tell inoffensive jokes or funny stories. Talk about anything good you have to say about shared friends or connections.

Some things are *never* small talk:

- Intimate relationships or sex

- Death
- Major medical problems like cancer or AIDS
- Personal gain that outpaces anyone else
- Business opportunities (especially sales or small business)
- Secrets (especially other peoples'). Also,

Some things *might* be taboo, so stay extremely mindful of everyone's responses:

- Age
- Weight
- Ethnic origin
- Marital or family status
- Salary and income
- Politics and social issues
- Religious views or philosophy
- The economy or the stock market
- Criticizing or patronizing someone's nationality or background (including some jokes)
- Any compliment that could be construed as flirting (usually by being more friendly than everyone normally would in the situation)

The point of small talk is for other people to feel safe with you on an unimportant thing to open a discussion you *do* find important. You will need plenty of patience, but it pays off.

Against your intuition, don't bring up topics you love until you've gained some experience. The point of small talk is to keep the subject light, so only address subjects you can accept dropping at the other person's convenience. Many great conversations have ground to a stop because the AS didn't want to shift subjects with the other person.

Don't try to steer small talk. People usually remember who first directed a conversation. They also feel important when you let *them* guide the topic.

Greeting People

The first seven seconds a person sees you defines their initial impression of you. Stand with your shoulders aligned with your neck and your back straight.

When people greet you, they form further impressions. The first few seconds talking with someone can define how that person sees you for months.

Most cultures use a greeting and farewell ritual, so memorize precisely how you want to greet and say goodbye. People need touch to feel a connection, usually with a firm but relenting handshake, but many Eastern cultures rarely or never use touch rituals. Maintain eye contact with the person through the entire greeting.

Many social groups have a distinct greeting format. Watch and copy everyone else. When you see multiple greeting styles, try to match someone else with a similar social position, age, and gender.

Mirroring

Closely mirror the people you talk to. Mirroring is a primal behavior of imitating people that says, "I'm like you". Most people aren't conscious of mirroring but act in response to it.

When someone changes a pose, delay matching them by about 20 seconds to a minute after them. If you can't mentally track your time, wait longer. If you mirror later than a minute or two NTs might feel you're not paying attention but doing it within 20 seconds will make them feel like you're trying to copy them.

If a person sits down, sit down with them. If they stand up, stand up. If they lean back, lean back. Match when they lean their face on their hand, lean forward, put their hand on a wall, and any other subtle gender-neutral body movements.

If someone keeps shifting their body or darting their eyes around the room, they're likely uncomfortable. Try to use what you know of them as a baseline to gauge where it comes from. They could have discomfort with you, the conversation or the environment. Change the subject to see if they ease up, then disengage the conversation if they persist.

Mirroring applies to facial expressions but at closer lagging intervals between 3 to 10 seconds afterward. You're simulating the speed they imagine you'll process their words. If they frown, frown. If they raise their eyebrows, raise your eyebrows. About every minute, use a different facial expression than them to prove you're not trying to deceive them.

As your conversation intensifies, mirror progressively faster to match the other person's speed. If they take longer to mirror or aren't mirroring you, they might not like you or don't want to continue the conversation. To test whether someone cares about you at all, perform a body gesture and watch if they match it.

Whenever someone makes a grand gesture, don't imitate that person's behavior. Instead, imitate *other responders'* behaviors to that person. As an example, someone who throws their arms up in frustration is symbolizing a type of "attack". Throwing your arms up in response is a type of "contest" to trigger their fight-or-flight reaction. Successful communicators respond with inaction ("I'm unaffected"), putting their hands at their sides ("I'll fight if I need, but don't want to") or pulling their arms close to their body ("you have power over me").

Personal Space

Don't touch someone unless you're certain they're okay with it. Don't shy away from other people trying to touch you. If someone touches you when you don't want it, say something like "I'm sorry, please don't touch me right now. I have a lot on my mind." If you're brave enough, you can say that social interactions are difficult for you. Vulnerability in the right context wins massive points with worthwhile people!

When meeting someone or talking to someone unfamiliar, stay anywhere from 4 to 12 feet away. If the person is a good friend or family member, you can close the distance up to about 18 inches. Any closer is an intimate zone for whispering in their ear with permission or touching.

Personal distance can move out of the 4 to 12-foot range for several reasons. People often stand closer to hear each other in a loud venue. People who feel familiar with each other draw close as well.

Several contexts ignore the 4-12' distance rule. Everyone generally ignores distance when they're working together on something mundane. People usually congregate in groups by standing together in a circle next to each other. Generally, romantic couples stand closer together at random intervals.

People often make more distance to signal that they want to leave the conversation. You'll notice by their feet pointing away from you and their body turned sideways.

The 4-foot distance rules fulfill a few purposes. First, the distance provides plenty of reaction time for an attack. Second, distance prevents us from smelling bad breath or body odor.

Generally, respect objects other people might use. Only dip chips once into a communal bowl chip dip. Leave the last piece of food unless you first ask everyone who may want it. Only grab second portions of food after everyone has the first helping. Flush after using the bathroom.

If you're in public, you're in a "common area". People in common areas have a "personal public space" about many small things. Unfortunately, you must learn the context of behavior in common areas through trial and error because each common area's rules consist of everyone's personal beliefs proportional to their power in the group.

Body Language

Observe who you turn from when you face anyone else. Align your body to who you're talking to while keeping your body aligned to everyone else you want to keep in the conversation. Pivot your upper head in a group to whoever is talking.

Don't look away unless you want to leave the conversation. If you look at something else for more than five seconds, that person will think you're done with the conversation. If the other person keeps looking away, they want to leave the conversation. If you see a distraction ahead of time (like a loud noise from something falling) look at it with the other person even if you don't see a need to.

If you can, turn your chair to face them while sitting. If you're using a table, keep the chair facing the table or angle it with the person and the table. When sitting in a chair you can't turn, pivot your torso toward them.

People express interest in someone when they point their toe at them. Point your toe at someone if they interest you. Watch their toes to see if they like you as well.

Fidgeting implies you want to "walk" away from the conversation, so avoid it and watch for it in others.

When doing a task, face the task and turn slightly toward the person you're talking to. Don't turn so far that it interferes with the work. Only talk while working when the other person is talking back. If someone is working and you aren't, avoid talking where it would distract them.

Be careful of sudden movements, especially ones that move toward people. It doesn't matter if you're far enough away that you won't touch them. Most NTs have instincts that react to all sudden movements as if it were a wild animal attacking. Try to avoid drawing attention with large gestures, flapping your hands or shaking your body.

In general, make your movements deliberate. You can compensate for AS' poor coordination by thinking ahead with premeditated gestures. I did well in high school sports by reacting to any movement from the corner of my eye. If possible, try to avoid careers that require rapid reflexes like first responders and military infantry.

AS naturally move from complete stillness through a rapid maneuver, but NTs need more "priming". Make fluid movements by slowly beginning the movement, transitioning to full speed, then slowing the movement to a stop. For example, get up from a chair by grabbing something (even if you won't use them), leaning into the movement, then slow down as you straighten your body. Warn people by looking at what you're about to do before you do it, especially if it crosses into another person's personal space.

Facial Expressions

Since the face is 10% of a body, an AS will logically conclude it contains 10% of the nonverbal cues. NTs see about 75% of nonverbal communication through the face, mostly in and around the eyes.

The rules of smooth movement also apply to facial expressions. Only make quick transitions in your face or eyes when you've become excited or shocked by something. NTs see any rapid facial transition without extreme feelings as a form of lying.

As an AS, facial expressions are the most challenging and rewarding. The slightest variation in muscle movement distinguishes between a wide range of feelings. For example, a smile can progress in intensity to convey satisfied, amused, happy, overjoyed, ecstatic, then manic.

Eye contact is challenging to master because it will stim you without practice. People usually don't notice if you alternate looking at their nose and mouth. Don't stare at their mouth much unless you want that person to think you're attracted to them.

Eye contact may be our greatest weakness, so don't ever expect to get it correct. All you need is to get it close enough to reliable that nobody feels it's out of place.

When talking with someone, look at their eyes or face about 85% of the time. Below 75% eye contact will make them think you're disinterested, but above 90% will make them think you distrust or plan to hurt them. Staring without looking away stims NTs from an animal instinct that you're hunting them.

Redirect the remaining 15% of eye contact in a circle away from them. I focused for months on repeating a cycle of left, then down, then right every 3-5 seconds. NTs usually move the circle inward as they intensify the conversation, so imitate inward movement when you're comfortable with the habit. For the greatest effect, synchronize breaks in eye contact with them saying something that provokes thought.

People often look one direction to recall memories, another to recall images, a third to form stories, and a fourth to form images. Vary the directions your eyes travel to show you're pulling from many sources of thought. I used to look hard to the right all the time until someone told me I looked like a compulsive liar.

Once you've become accustomed to eye contact, avoid stimming by learning to stare at people without perceiving. If you've accustomed yourself to moving your eyes around, most NTs won't be able to tell.

Your ideas will distract people from your body language, but not your face. Your face gives them context for what they should feel. If your eyes dart around, they'll think you're concentrating or are uncomfortable. If an NT's eyes dart around, they want to leave the conversation.

Never stare at some things, not even absentmindedly! Looking at someone's body part, especially if they have a physical disability, will make them think you have a problem with it. Only stare at someone for more than a few seconds if you want to get their attention, even from across the room. You can only stare at the opposite gender's chest or butt if that person has already reciprocated from your direct romantic effort.

To express feelings, exaggerate your face to convey them through the region around your eyes. AS tend to under-express compared to NTs, so magnifying your facial expressions will give context for how people should feel around you.

Learn to smile when you're happy. Practice in the mirror until it feels photogenic and natural. A natural smile uses all the facial muscles and should show crow's feet at the sides of the eyes.

One-on-one settings are the correct time to express negative feelings like sadness and anger, but not in groups that don't directly confront those feelings. Don't express stronger feelings than the rest of a group. If someone looks sad, don't smile unless you're trying to cheer them up. If everyone looks happy, don't express sadness or discouragement. If the group seems to have mixed feelings or is talking about two or more subjects, it broke into sub-groups when you weren't paying attention.

If you're in a big group, pay attention to where other people are looking. They're often observing another person or group and became disinterested at that moment with what you were saying. Don't take it personally and drop the subject. I know you want to keep on that subject but trust me when I say that you *must* drop it if you want to continue your relationship with them. You'll have plenty of opportunities to share with them later in the unforeseeable future.

Observe and learn how to express specific moods. You've likely been misinformed in how you appear. My growing-up years expressed "rage" when I actually meant to convey "distress"!

Be careful with laughter. Inappropriate laughter can devastate a reputation. If you can scale the laughter down to a smile, you won't get in trouble for it. Think of something either tragic or painful when you need to stifle your laughter. If you observe something funny when nobody wants to hear it, write it down and share it later. Present-tense pain is usually tragic while past-tense pain is often funny.

Speaking

Speech sends far more information than text. People understand ideas through many parts of speech. NTs watch how someone pronounces words, speaking speed, volume, choice of words, emphasis on specific words, and the words' relationship to other nearby statements and words.

Try to analyze the different parts of speech and how they can change implications. The more you understand the mechanics of speech and language, the easier you'll follow what everyone else is feeling.

Time your speaking to not interrupt anyone else. Let a few seconds of silence persist before responding to make sure. When responding, always start your sentence with either a summary of their idea or a transition modifier like "speaking of which..." or "now that you mention it..."

Only transition to something unrelated to their statement by requesting to change the subject. Sometimes, related ideas to you are completely unrelated to others, but you'll only discover that by trial and error.

Because people want to feel important, learn to ask more questions. Express curiosity in something they like or do. If you can't find anything, try to discover what they like or don't like, then work off that. If you learned more about someone than they did about you, they'll feel more important and, naturally, will like you more.

Some people run their sentences together back-to-back or only want someone to listen to them speak. Either learn how to interrupt them when they conclude an idea or find someone else to talk to.

AS often ignore their volume, especially when they're excited about a subject. Speak so your listener can hear you but nobody else can. Always match your voice to the environment, not to the person you're speaking to.

Watch your voice pattern. Many AS project their emotional energy by beginning sentences loudly, but NTs are usually unsettled by it. Start your first word quietly, then keep a consistent volume throughout.

When you're finished with a sentence, pause for a half a second. End your statement by moving the tone upward for a question or downward for everything else. Let silence persist once you've finished your thought. 95% of the things you say will be original ideas to an NT, so be patient while they process it.

Always incorporate the other person's thoughts and opinions into your statements! A conversation is a back-and-forth exchange. People are reading far more than you realize, so learn to be more concise and considerate of their time.

Your ability to listen is your most critical communication skill. If you can quote or paraphrase what someone said, they know you were listening to them. Focus on remembering their ideas more than their words.

People find you interesting when you decrease how much you speak. This is counter-intuitive, even to most NTs! By listening, you show them that they're important to you. Everyone needs to feel important. Our understanding of meaning and purpose comes through how we feel important. Try to talk less than 50% of the time, then aim for less than 30%.

Scale your proportion of speaking to the group's size. If you're with two people, limit yourself to 33% of the time. With three people, 25% of the time, four people at 20% of the time, and so on.

When you find someone with the same interests as you, most of them will be less interested in it than you. Respect their desires and keep the conversation as light and casual as they want. Discuss more in-depth if they want to stay on the subject but get ready to drop it and move to whatever they bring up.

Some NTs will revisit a previous subject, but *never* try to steer the conversation back to a past topic. The NT very likely knows you love that topic and doesn't want to talk about it.

If the topic moves outside your interest or knowledge, ask questions instead. You're talking about *their* interest, so don't share what you know. Never correct them unless they ask you for advice, even when they're completely wrong or misguided. Everyone has the right to believe what they want, even if it's wrong, and you can dismiss yourself if you don't want to hear it anymore.

Be curious about what that person likes. Find creative ways to intersect what you both enjoy. For example, you may like cars while the other person likes bicycle races. The two fields have plenty of similarities and differences to fill a long conversation.

Most people have no issue with what you say, but often how you say it. Generally, add fillers like "this is just my opinion, but…", "I don't know if you'd agree, but…", and "While this may come across as rude…" It prepares people for a possible blow and you'll see immediate improvements in your engagements.

Getting accustomed to shifting topics is difficult. AS find most topics boring and deep fascination with a few. You can only survive in the NT world with bite-sized chunks of what you like. After searching long enough, you'll find others who share your passions. Unfortunately, finding those people is a matter of happenstance, so never stop meeting new people!

If you do find someone who shares your passion, don't let the opportunity to connect slip by. If you're at a social event, swap contact information and find someone else to mingle with. Healthy networking strikes at opportunities while they're available. Build on them later when the event has passed.

If you're telling a story, only give details that support a one-sentence main idea. AS often give a plethora of details that confuse the listener.

For example, if you're talking about how you discovered the venue, don't say:

"My friend Bob knows Tim who runs this event, and two weeks ago he bugged me for the 31st time to come to this. I finally relented and am now here."

Instead, say:

"My friend Bob, you might know him, was interested in it, so I came here after he kept bugging me."

Keep some things unstated. Err on the side of silence. Try to only say things a politician would say. Never say anything that would offend someone within earshot.

You can't completely avoid offending people. You'll sometimes learn inappropriate statements the hard way. If you can learn how to never make the same mistake twice, you'll grow from it regardless.

Facing Rejection

You will mess up. When you do, learn to fail well. Use humor at your expense. When I see disapproving faces from failing one of the rules, I often say "oh, *that's* how humans do it!" Other times, if everyone is comfortable enough, I'll blame my lack of coordination on a flat surface. If you don't feel comfortable with humor, transition the focus to something else. If people press you on it, apologize without qualifiers and promise to not do it again.

People communicate they're done talking in more ways than swaying, making distance, and darting their eyes around the room. They'll set objects between both of you. You'll begin noticing a specific tone of voice that indicates the stress pattern when people feel uncomfortable.

People leave conversations without explanation for a variety of reasons. Sometimes you've been offensive. Other times they don't want to risk rudely cutting off the conversation but have other things to do. They might have appointments to keep or want to meet other people at the same event. That person could be an introvert and get as drained from social experiences as you!

Most NTs are terrible at ending a conversation they don't like if someone didn't notice their hints. The correct way is to say something to the effect of "Excuse me, I have to go." They'll usually fabricate a reason to leave. That reason will usually be a lie about something they want to do or why they must leave. You'll learn to spot their lies, but don't call them out. If they cared about their relationship with you, they'd be honest.

If you detect social distance, don't follow them or wait for them to finish what they said they'd do. If you feel any uncertainty, trust it and move on to someone else. People often lie, so don't presume everything they say as fact. Frequently ask *why* they'd say something to understand them more.

If *you're* having trouble staying in the conversation, tell them that you must go. If you're staying at that venue, look for someone else familiar and say you want to talk to that person before you leave. Since you'd rather talk to that person than who you're talking to, you're not lying.

Processing This

Once you're aware of how much NTs lie, you have every reason to become bitter. I imagine every AS must battle it before they can integrate into society.

The cure for bitterness is to focus on good things and move on from the bad. Though average people are lame, great people are still worth your investment. Spending extra time thinking of the people you like the least will give them power over you.

As you develop social skills, your opinions of friends and associates will vacillate. Before long, some people that had rejected you will go out of their way to connect with you. You'll also likely lose some lifelong friends as you out-achieve them.

Keep making theories about how people work. Some of your theories will get complicated. Within a few short years, your theories will be about 95% as reliable as what NTs use! Of course, you'll *know* how social behaviors work instead of their gut intuition, so consider that an advantage.

This journey isn't easy. I've given you *what* to do, but not much on *how* to overcome your greatest hurdles. The next chapter focuses on how to reach your goals.

Your Hardest Struggles

For AS to accept and conform to the HIS, we must face a few battles at the same time. There aren't any simple solutions, but you can overcome most of them with well-focused habits. Changing habits is difficult, but the rewards are worth it.

1: Stimming

Even when you can follow all the rules, you *will* face sensory overload. You'll have stim reactions. Most of them will be unacceptable in public. Avoid anything that drags you below that 90% HIS including barking, yelling or rocking back and forth.

You can't avoid stimming, but you *can* accommodate it by observing and avoiding nervous breakdowns before they happen. This takes practice and self-awareness.

We stim when we can't process mental information fast enough. Some triggers are many small elements at once (crinkling paper, swarming ants, specific textures, TV static). Other triggers drain our ability to think (decision-making, loud noises, things competing for our attention).

Adapt your lifestyle to accommodate your weaknesses. NTs do it all the time, so you can too! Avoid concerts if you hate large crowds, find indoor or urban hobbies if nature overwhelms you, avoid anything you fear.

Of course, we can't avoid some things. We still must go to work and school, attend church, do our chores, cook our food, run our errands. If you can't avoid the experience, dedicate personal time to build a resistance to it. No matter how overwhelming, you can train your mind like a muscle to transition into situations.

These limits are your opportunity to find creative solutions! In my own life, I watched back-to-back videos of concerts until I became accustomed to the thousands of movements in crowds. Though I still struggle with visual stimuli, I've compensated by learning how to stare like I'm focused, but without processing it.

You'll never eradicate your stimming. When you encounter a trigger, travel to a predetermined "safe place" as soon as possible. Politely excuse yourself to avoid further stimming from others noticing you. The bathroom is the easiest spot because it's quieter than the venue, consistent, usually available, and you can use it every few hours without others getting concerned.

Most AS stall stimming by manipulating something or "scripting" quotes. As you get better at coping, try downsizing the scope of what you're doing. If you hold a deck of cards, move to a card or miniature deck. Replace uncommon items with commonplace items. Use simpler quotes that are less conspicuous. I had to transition through holding a yo-yo, a collectible coin, spinning my wedding ring, picking at my nails, and finally twiddling my thumbs. I also went from quoting lines from textbooks to saying, "it's all good" and "works for me!", and now I just quietly say "hmmm".

If you're stuck stimming somewhere you can't leave, have a predefined expression. I often look like I'm thinking to hide when I'm overwhelmed. Try to fixate on an immovable object to bring some much-needed security. When you have experience focusing, transition to thinking of philosophical constants beyond the physical world.

You *can* remove the social effects of stimming even if you don't remove the triggers. As you become more comfortable with people, you'll notice a stronger tolerance for uncertainties and overload.

If an NT doesn't give you grace over your weakness, they're oblivious to themselves. An NT in a room with the heater on full-blast, bright strobe lights, and 15 unrelated songs playing at 110 dB would be as stimmed as any AS.

2: Anger at Stupid Social Rules

Working hard to follow rules you don't like to please people is often irritating. It's maddening when you don't understand where they come from or why they exist. Even with tons of experience, we'll never "get it".

I've honored most of the HIS rules for about a decade and researched quite a few of them. Society made most rules canon *long* before we were born. If you investigate where most of them came from, they had a purpose at one point but make no sense now.

Further, the rules are often petty. Some apply to specific contexts or one-time circumstances. Others come through or for specific cultures. While some groups don't care if you break most of them, others will excommunicate you from one minor infraction.

Most people only understand the rules through subconscious intuition. Almost all the rules are variations or suppressions of animal instincts. Some rules accommodate people suffering from past trauma. The most inconvenient social rules are designed to circumvent irrational fears.

The social rules are an unspoken agreement to give a sandboxed "test zone" for people to verify others' trustworthiness. This system mislabels all AS as dangerous who don't get that 85% HIS Score.

We have no choice. AS won't become acceptable with "autism awareness" campaigns. People may become aware of autism, but they won't automatically become more patient with you. In fact, this added "awareness" about AS has generated enough myths that I think it's hurting us more than helping!

The solution is to prove that you can succeed. You have high-quality knowledge in your mind right now and society needs to hear it. The only way we can change this HIS is by adapting it from the inside. I'd *love* for us to scrap everything to form a more rational system from the ground up. Unfortunately, every attempt at a universal human *anything* are stories of failure, mostly because people are resistant to change.

3: Discrepant Behavior

Some specific people will stim you as soon as you look at them. Something will feel...off about them. They might say they care while their eyes show rage. They might lean in for a hug while their body is stiff. They will ask you to trust them while you can tell they distrust you.

You've discovered a discrepant human being. These people give tremendous trouble to an AS. Some of them are mentally unstable while others have Narcissistic Personality Disorder (NPD). They represent a significant minority of the planet. While they're more frequently in religion and politics, many of them scrape their way into leadership everywhere.

Some people are always discrepant while others only do it occasionally. People are inconsistent for three major reasons:

Reason 1 – They want you to like them but can't be honest with themselves. They're trying to avoid hurting your feelings but also don't like you. If they were honest with themselves, they'd dislike you, but they've spent so much time communicating vaguely that they can't even *think* straight! Your mental life is far easier than theirs. Don't waste your time trying to understand them.

Reason 2 – They like you but get offended by you. People often like your ideas while finding something about your behavior offensive. They're anxious because they don't know how to confront you. If you sense their anxiety, they can often tell you know and will become more anxious. Don't be afraid to express your feelings with them, but don't expect openness in return.

Reason 3 – Their personality is literally split apart. Some people have gigantic walls between what they're thinking and what they're doing. Watch for a jittery and uneasy disposition they seem to carry even when they're not talking to anyone. Avoid these people.

Whatever you do, don't let them stim you. These people are usually obsessed with their public image. If they see you in a moment of weakness, they might shame you to redirect attention away from themselves.

In any of these cases, the safest decision is to give them distance. Avoid them or go somewhere away from them. Observe how they behave with others from a distance, then try to engage them in private to see if they've improved. If you are related to or work for one, try to spend as little time with that person as possible.

4: Nobody Seems to Care!

AS usually have abandonment issues. They'll feel like nobody cares about them or their ideas. I can testify to two decades of feeling completely alone with nobody to talk to or share life with.

What you're feeling is far more severe than reality. What you may feel is rejection from others is very often that they're confused. Most NTs get intimidated by what they don't understand.

Your thoughts will be alien to NTs, even the ones you're friends with. Look for people you can trust. Though the world won't understand you, the few people who care to learn about you are worth your investment. Acceptance doesn't need understanding.

You may have a long time until you find someone who identifies with you. Most NTs feel like nobody fully understands them. Since AS are a unique and eclectic group, you may never find someone who shares how you think.

The topical, bottom-up nature of AS thinking forms into extremely specialized preferences. While you won't find complete synchronous thinking with anyone, each person has *something* in common with you!

Keep working hard at whatever you excel at. You can relate to others in that field and have something to show for your time. Your successes will draw successful people to you. Learning social rules ensures you'll become sophisticated enough that nobody will ever detect your autism.

Making It Stick

Our connections with others are the only way we can thrive. It's also how we reap from our success.

You need a networked group to find a place in society. Choose people that give both encouragement and constructive criticism. Try a church, club or anywhere else where people meet. Only attend groups that encourage you and draw you out of your comfort zone. Try to find groups with people who lead it that have succeeded *more* than you.

Keep testing groups to find one where you can meet its needs and it can meet yours. Cycle through many groups if you need to. Each new group is a chance to learn and retry. I've cycled through about 23 networks so far and *still* find people who expand my view of the world!

You probably use Reddit, Facebook, Twitch or some other social network, but don't limit yourself to online-only. We need in-person connections, but it takes consistent practice to hold a real-life conversation. Use social networks like Meetup and Craigslist as a springboard for face-to-face encounters.

Social skills are completely trainable. The most successful people, in any attempt, weren't the best qualified. Instead, they poured their willpower into building their skills for years. This requires faith in yourself. Aim for adequacy, not perfection. Get input from other successes. Read any popular books on social skills. I made a website (https://adequate.life) on what to do and another one (https://gainedin.site) on why.

If you're on the AS, you can build amazing things! You might be able to craft an entire fictional world with intricate detail. You could be the engineer that solves the world's food or energy crisis. You could develop an algorithm that magnifies data transfer. Neurotypicals must exhaust themselves to get to your level of natural talent. The only barrier to your success is that HIS Score!

The greatest social accomplishment as an AS is when the NTs don't notice. For myself, I knew I'd arrived when I stopped hearing constructive criticism that I was "awkward" or "overbearing". Shortly after, people started saying my ideas were "rational" or "creative". Now, people are fascinated by me and I'm fast becoming moderately influential!

If you succeed as AS, people who know you well will completely forget you're someone with special needs. Once an NT confuses you as another NT, you've outranked the average person in aptitude because of where you started. Overcoming the downsides of AS will make you more focused, regimented, determined, straightforward, and analytical than most of your peers. If you can avoid reminding people that you're on the spectrum, you can be as unique and adventurous as you want! Thousands of others already have!

Appendix A: Famous AS

- Hans Christian Andersen
- Dan Aykroyd
- Marty Balin
- Benjamin Banneker (probably)
- Susan Boyle
- Dan Aykroyd
- Tim Burton
- Lewis Carroll
- Henry Cavendish (probably)
- Charles Darwin (probably)
- Tony DeBlois
- Emily Dickinson
- Paul Dirac (probably)
- Albert Einstein (probably)
- Bobby Fischer
- Bill Gates
- Temple Grandin
- Daryl Hannah
- James Hobley
- Thomas Jefferson (probably)
- Steve Jobs
- Linus Torvalds (probably)
- James Joyce (probably)
- Stanley Kubrick
- Courtney Love
- Caiseal Mór
- Wolfgang Amadeus Mozart (probably)

- Michelangelo (probably)
- Isaac Newton (probably)
- Matt Savage
- Jerry Seinfeld
- Satoshi Tajiri
- Nikola Tesla (probably)
- Andy Warhol
- Ludwig Wittgenstein (probably)
- William Butler Yeats (probably)

Appendix B: Socially Skilled AS Advantages

- Detail-minded makes analysis easier when trained
- Niche-mindedness creates opportunities to transform society at the margins
- Easier to recover from hardship because triggers are highly localized to specific circumstances
- Extreme focus and dedication to projects makes highly productive work for long durations
- Neural splinters/savants have unusually exceptional talents that are usually cross-trainable to other disciplines
- Low social interaction allows long hours at a task without human connection
- Need for rhythm and consistency empowers rigorous discipline with clear boundaries
- Obsession with details allows for highly technical work
- Disregard for social standards allows unconventional and creative thought
- Can find meaning in seemingly mundane tasks

Don't miss out!

Visit the website below and you can sign up to receive emails whenever Greg Stucky publishes a new book. There's no charge and no obligation.

https://books2read.com/r/B-A-GYFK-ACJEB

BOOKS 2 READ

Connecting independent readers to independent writers.

Did you love *How to Stop Looking Autistic*? Then you should read *How to Start Looking at Autism*[1] by Greg Stucky!

Have you heard about autism but don't know what it is?Does your child exhibit signs of autism, but you're not sure what to believe?Do you have a hard time around friends, coworkers or family that you suspect might be in the spectrum?This quick guide to autism is written with you in mind.After reading this book you'll not only understand how autistics think, but also how to engage with and succeed with them.

Read more at https://stucky.tech.

---

1. https://books2read.com/u/b68zn0

2. https://books2read.com/u/b68zn0

Also by Greg Stucky

Autism
How to Start Looking at Autism
How to Stop Looking Autistic

Philosophy
TL;DR Philosophy

Watch for more at https://stucky.tech.

www.ingramcontent.com/pod-product-compliance
Lightning Source LLC
Chambersburg PA
CBHW031421160726

47993CB00003B/1337